WHAT AM I?

The fun animal guessing book!

by

Lisa Kishtwari

This book belongs to:

....

In the beginning…God created the great creatures of the sea according to their kinds, and every winged bird according to its kind…
And God said, "Let the land produce living creatures according to their kinds: the livestock, the creatures that move along the ground, and the wild animals, each according to its kind…" And God saw that it was good.

Genesis Chapter 1

People think I'm **scary**,
big and **sharp** are my teeth.
My fin can show above the water
while my body **lurks** beneath!

WHAT AM I?

I'm a SHARK!

FUN FACT:
The most dangerous shark
is the Great White shark.

I can **dive** really deep
and have skin that feels like **rubber**.
I can live in the bitter cold
because of my **thick** blubber!

WHAT AM I?

I'm a
SEAL!

FUN FACT:
Seals can hold their breath
for nearly 2 hours.

I have **wings** but I cannot fly,
I eat fish, squid and krill.
To keep warm in the **bitter** cold,
I **huddle** nice and still!

WHAT AM I?

I'm a PENGUIN!

FUN FACT:
Penguins spend most of
their time in the water.

I'm black with white markings,
and I live in the sea.
I am the biggest dolphin;
I hunt seals for my tea!

WHAT AM I?

I'm an ORCA!

FUN FACT:
Orcas are found in all the
oceans of the world.

I am able to **change** colour
and my **grip** on trees is strong.
My eyes can move in all directions,
my tongue is **sticky** and long!

WHAT AM I?

I live in the **rainforest**,
and have a very large beak.
My colours are really **dazzling**;
fruit is mainly what I eat!

WHAT AM I?

I'm a
TOUCAN!

FUN FACT:
Toucans are very noisy birds.

I'm a very **graceful** swimmer
but move clumsily on **land**:
I can live for 100 years;
I lay my **eggs** in the sand!

WHAT AM I?

I'm a TURTLE!

FUN FACT:
Females return to the same beach
where they hatched, to lay their eggs.

I like to walk in **water**,
I **hatched** from an egg.
My feathers are pink in colour;
I often stand on **one** leg!

WHAT AM I?

I'm a
FLAMINGO!

FUN FACT:
Flamingoes have pink feathers
because of the pink shrimps they eat.

My nose is really **long**
and my **tail** is very dinky.
I flap my ears – that keeps me cool;
my skin looks **super** wrinkly!

WHAT AM I?

I'm an
ELEPHANT!

FUN FACT:
An elephant uses its trunk as a snorkel
when it swims.

I live in the **rainforests**,
my colours are bright.
I like to **croak** loudly
when I come out at night!

WHAT AM I?

I'm a
TREE FROG!

FUN FACT:
Baby tree frogs are brown in colour.

Mark and Kay Holland,

who always encourage us to be ourselves.

opyright © Majestic Whale Encounters

uthors: Sarah Cullen & Carmen Ellis

rtwork & Book Design © Zuzana Svobodová

le: Spike, the penguin with rainbow hair

BN 978-0-6488498-5-8 (Paperback)

BN 978-0-6488498-4-1 (Hardcover)

BN 978-0-6488498-3-4 (eBook)

I'm a **strange** kind of creature,
I have fins, gills, a tail.
I live in water **and** on land;
my body is covered in scales!

WHAT AM I?

I'm a MUDSKIPPER!

FUN FACT:
Mudskippers are a fish that
can breathe in and out of water.

I live in a **big** family
and we **sleep** in the ground.
We take turns to look for danger
by **standing** upright on a mound!

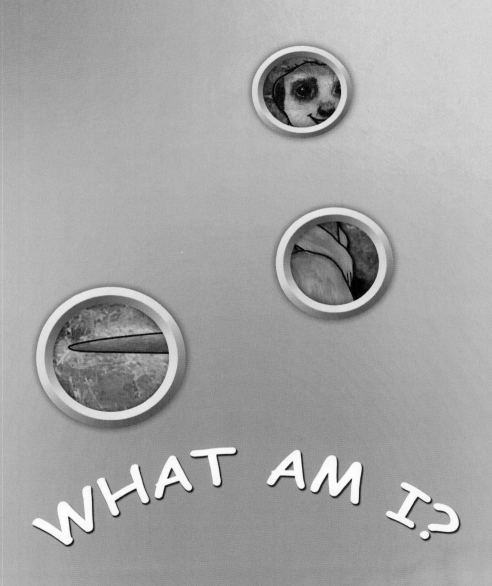

WHAT AM I?

I'm a
MEERKAT!

FUN FACT:
Meerkats can close their
ears when they are burrowing to
keep out dirt.

I move really slowly
and for many hours I doze.
My fur is very shaggy;
I have big claws instead of toes!

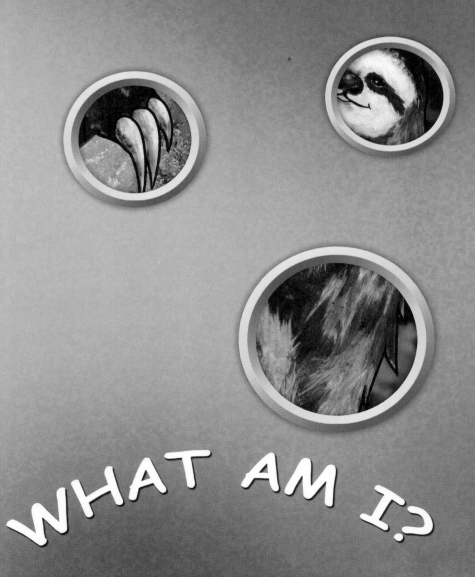

WHAT AM I?

I'm a SLOTH!

FUN FACT:
Sloths spend 10 hours of the daytime sleeping.

I became extinct years ago,
I had sharp **teeth** in my beak.
I had wings but no feathers;
I flew around finding things to **eat**!

WHAT AM I?

I'm a
PTERODACTYL!

FUN FACT:
Pterodactyls had about 90 teeth
in their beaks.

Although I have wings I cannot fly;
I hatched from a **very** large egg.
I can run faster than any of you
because of my **powerful** legs!

WHAT AM I?

I'm an OSTRICH!

FUN FACT:
The ostrich is the largest living bird.

I'm a type of **African** animal,
I graze in the sun.
I'm very **quick** on my feet;
I twist and turn as **I run!**

WHAT AM I?

I'm an
IMPALA!

FUN FACT:
Impalas can leap more than 3
times their height.

I live in the outback
where it's dry and very hot.
I have a pouch on my tummy;
I can't walk – instead, I hop!

WHAT AM I?

I'm a
KANGAROO!

FUN FACT:
Kangaroos carry their babies
around in a pouch on their tummies.

All things bright and beautiful,
all creatures great and small,
all things wise and wonderful,
the Lord God made them all.*

* Cecil Frances Alexander (1848)

Books by the authors

Available to buy on Amazon

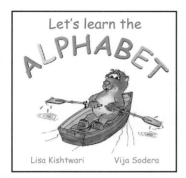

This beautifully illustrated and amusing book will help children to learn the alphabet, and also the names of many different animals.

'Let's learn to count' is available in several other languages including Spanish, Hindi, Japanese, Ukrainian, Yoruba & more.

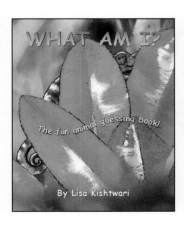
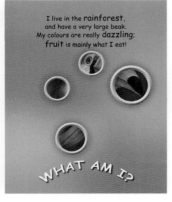

Young children can have fun guessing the animals with the help of a rhyme, and with visual clues showing different parts of the animal.

Scan this QR code to view these books on **Amazon**.

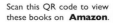

For Rio & Jasmeena

Written, illustrated & produced by Lisa Kishtwari

one small
Mango books

Printed in Great Britain
by Amazon

28303940R00025